HEAVENLY BODIES AT THE MET

ELLEN DEVLIN

Červená Barva Press
Somerville, Massachusetts

Červená Barva Press
P.O. Box 440357
W. Somerville, MA 02144-3222

www.cervenabarvapress.com

Bookstore: www.thelostbookshelf.com

Cover art and design: Hugh Scully

ISBN: 978-1-950063-57-4

ACKNOWLEDGMENTS

I would like to thank Gloria Mindock, editor and publisher of Červená Barva Press for her continuing support and for publishing "Heavenly Bodies." I also thank Flower Conroy, Gillian Cummings, and Anne Graue for their editing assistance.

TABLE OF CONTENTS

HEAVENLY BODIES AT THE MET

Guadalupe, Evening Dress

Jean Paul Gaultier, designer

Grieving mother Mary
your silk heart sheaths
a small metal dagger

blue-jersey beauty Mary
you draw us close
make us yearn for you

who doesn't want a mother
who pierces her own heart
for us pours out

her silk blood red shimmering
wet as if it just happened
as if it has always just happened

Crown of Thorns, Headpiece

Shawn Leane, designer/silversmith

with silver thorns
the crown fills our eyes
filed to blunt barbs

angled away
from the wearer's head—
made for adornment

what can be done with this torture
remaking
sometimes we twist the thorns
from the tender skin
of the other

Ex-Voto, Evening Ensemble

Jean Paul Gaultier, designer

What happens when we wear
or ex-votos—
tin metal hearts
loaves of bread
small wooden paintings of our children
stitched to a silk dress
we wore everyday copper lace
holding fast so that when we moved
we felt the small weight tapping
reminders of our childrens' broken
bones healed   our house rising
after a fire   flood found
when none
could be found

Ensemble

John Galliano, designer

Warrior queen lying in state
do you keep or forget

linden trees combed by sunlight
and the flight of crows

what do the dead want
carrying their swords or babies

or the pear they were eating
into the abyss

warrior queen lying in state
silver-threaded

black-silk-gowned
a crystal crown of sea horses

one side of your body armored
one open—

nothing protected you
floating forever now

buried in the detritus
of ocean floor sightless

is sound a silver-handled mirror
is almond the taste of stillness

Undercover

Jun Takahaski, designer

printed on a silk mini dress
The Garden of Earthly Delights
desire exhaling a soft *o*
opens mouths
berries dropped by birds
fall on tongues
that reach and splay
open eggs birthing
arms and legs slick
with sweat and sap
of orchids no rinds
or refusal
all orifice flowering pleasure
in face and flanks
gears of the world turning

Coat Dress

Alexander McQueen, designer

A panel glows on the right side
of the skirt silk-printed detail
The Last Judgment—

the woman in the coat dress says
he will come again to judge
the living and the dead

a gold-winged bronze-armored
archangel holds a scale weighing souls
drives the damned to hell with his sword

his face is oddly aloof as if he were
weighing pears simply interested
in the math of the calculation

this woman is all business—zipper
of her high-collared coatdress
glittering metal teeth fierce as her posture

and I am remembering the terrible
weight of fear its dailiness in prayers
catechism lessons stained glass

Ensemble

Jean Paul Gaultier, designer

I kept walking past you
sign that read *Joan of Arc*
avoiding your young face
light hair resting on a pillow
your dead body slight unbearable
the white chemise didn't reach
your bare feet—
a satin corset bound your torso
it's garter tabs lying on your thin legs
one sleeve of plate armor

Dress

Azzedine Alaia, designer

Made to be worn
for the ritual cleansing
of inherited sin
from other parents
who only wanted
to taste Eden to know
good and evil

white cotton and silk
soft pleated long-sleeved
modest baptismal required

how can this be? babies
come into the world
continuing

Ensemble

Rick Owens, designer

A monk's robe brown broadcloth
a hole cut
in the tunic
below the waist

I was 13 kneeling in a confessional
you asked me
where I was touched
on which parts of my body

how many times

I stopped answering

you leaned your sweat-slicked
head into the lattice window between us
The wet-wool smell of your cassock

your cigarette breath pushed
into the small divide
between us

I had no name
for the cold fear your anticipation
breathed through my body

Evening Ensemble

Pierpaolo Piccioli and Grazia Churri, designers

Black silk cape embroidered
with gold stars contours

of a cassock on a woman's body
this confessor opens

the lattice screen takes my hands
in hers and fill them with her necklace

the gold band around her hair
to wear in holy joy the next time

I invite touch

this is my body

Cocktail Dress

Gabrielle "Coco" Chanel, designer

I know the iconography
of wheat stalks on the gold

silk gown
its embroidered auricles
wrapping the stem

where sheath meets leaf
gold-painted feathers

lift and sway at the shoulders
I think *bread of life*

I do not believe
or disbelieve
bread blessed has the presence of god

food is enough
it doesn't matter
sharing bread is enough

Ensemble

Vandervorst and Aricks, designers

Inspired by bishops' dress
but finer fit
to a woman's body—
a small fuchsia sash
elegance of hip widening
narrow fall   of black silk

Wedding Ensemble

Cristobel Balenciaga, designer

I have been this bride
soft circles of veil and gardenia
this is how to begin
in the church that houses
the devotion of my ancestors
here nested
in my parent's hopes
poinsettias evergreen garlands

I was alone
swathed in white silk
a mournful *Ave Maria*
the pointy toes of my shoes
caught twice on my dress
Do I want this pulsing
against the seed pearl headpiece

there's a tradition
of the bride leaving her bouquet
at Mary's altar
ringed and wed I gave the flowers
to my mother Skirts rustled
throats cleared
my mother startled
leaned back from my kiss
it snowed that day

Wedding Ensemble

Tom Browne, designer

Meadow flowers root and runnel

as the unicorn surrenders to a fenced round

he could easily breach

allows the white chain

to bind him

to the pomegranate tree

mink skirted tulle breath

I agree to be his bride

Ensemble

Tom Browne, designer

It was April a finch was singing
from a tree with a small birdhouse
nailed to its trunk

I spent years with you Sister
came only as close
as the sound of your
skirt moving across the floor

you returned
in this black cape
your nose and mouth swathed
in white lamb's wool

and again I was object
you interrogator

what were you looking for
in my unbrushed hair
the silence
you required of rooms

a little girl crying
for her mother pulling
at a door you locked

ran to you clawed
at your skirts buried her face
in your untouchable
volume

you beat her with a closed fist
pushing the wide arc of your sleeves
up your arms

the floor was gray
and yellow tiled
in the corner small table
with three chairs
the walls were green

Evening Ensemble

Pierpaolo Picciola, designer

Among all the imagined nuns'
habits I knew
which one was you—

the black cashmere dress
jewel collar
long sleeves
a panel of ivory silk falling
from the yoke
to the floor—
not your actual habit
but your essence—
no excess
no hard edges

I was eight
you've stayed
with me I see you when I write

Evening Ensemble

John Galliano, designer

Boys dressed in red tunics
sat on a wall outside the museum
dangling rosary beads
like fishing lines
600 in all gathered in protest
some came by bus some joined in
on the way back from the grocery store
they leaned against police gates
prayed sang hymns offended
by a MET exhibit of a woman's body
dressed in papal regalia
tiara mozetta cassock
delicate shoulders
bust line
and the fullness of women hips

Evening Dress

Alexander McQueen, designer

Archangel messenger Gabriel
silk screened on a gray gown

the front of a woman's body holds
his resolute face his hand lifted
in a gesture that says *edict*

her back holds his wings
shoulder to ankle
powered by the breath of god

Evening Dress

Dolce and Gabbana, designers

In tesserae on a Byzantium wall

or polychrome crystals on a dress

gather your stone tiles

and make of her image

an amendment

she remains gold leaf

without your consent

her luminous softness

is wholly hers

Dress

Alexander McQueen, designer

This mini dress
 imprinted with Boch's Hell—
frog demons sauté human parts
in frying pans
birds with snouts
dunk naked sinners
in melted metal coins

I turn away
turn back
an oily fear in my throat—

remember my child's terror
of a child's sins
sealing my sleep
with nightmares

Evening Dress

Oliver Theyskens, designer

Black silk moiré
dress a cross
cut from neck to waist
shoulder to shoulder

hook and eye closures
grapple
with exposure
concealment
gather the borders

of crossbar and stake
the double wish
for her desire
and impaling

Breastplate

Alexander McQueen and Shaun Leane, designers

a breastplate molded
to a woman's torso
among the museum's other reliquaries

silver roses abundant bloom
from her shoulders
cross breasts and hips
with botanical precision—

the casing of her holiness
the beating heart of a living woman

Evening Dress

Churri and Picciolo, designers

This is my body
my silken birthright

sieve me for sin
and fragrant apples

bee-studded trees
all of Eden is here—

lustrous bodies of Adam and Eve
embroidered in colored silk

reach for each other
vines and woodland creatures

spins from threads
across gold butterflies

and I feel my skin
and flowering breath

desire is a holy engine
as much blossom as snake

Evening Dress

Valentino, designer

gold crosses red gown's soft oval
cut to mid-torso
women dressed as Princes of the Church

raise themselves
to redeem the world

all our birthing blood is here
and the blood of beating rape soaking
the bishops' gown for centuries

conferred at the beginning
as stewards of mystery
they were the chosen ones

all the bending of bones

they anoint each other's heads

While we are here
with our lives lived
on low ground
in fear and excrement

Statuary Vestment for the Madonna Della Grazie

Poor Benedictine Nuns of Lecce, designers

1.
As if you were not enough
carved from butter wood
set high above your altar
in the church named for you—
you were dressed by nuns
in a blue silk mantle
a skyscape of embroidered stars
your ivory silk gown flowering
vines of gold passementerie
a silver crown with gold cherubs
placed on your head

2.
Our Lady of Graces
how sure of your favor
petitioners must've been
lighting the red votive candles
placed before you how willing
to leave their coins
in the metal box

3.
there is so much hope
in the dilation of the human eye
when gazing at crystals
and gold thread

NOTES

From May 10 to October 8, 2018, 1,659,647 people visited the costume exhibit, *Heavenly Bodies: Fashion and the Catholic Imagination* at the Metropolitan Museum of Art, making it the most visited exhibit in the history of the MET.

The poems in this collection were all responses to the couture exhibited in "Heavenly Bodies: Fashion and the Catholic Imagination " at the Metropolitan Museum of Art, NY, NY May-October, 2018. The designers and dates of the collections are listed here:

Guadalupe: *Jean Paul Gaultier, designer (spring/summer2007)*.

Crown of Thorns, headpiece: *Shawn Leane, designer, silversmith for Alexander McQueen (autumn/winter 1996-79)*.

Ex-Voto, Evening Ensemble: Jean *Paul Gaultier, designer (spring/summer, 2007)*.

Ensemble: *John Galliano, designer (autumn /winter, 2011-2012)*.

Undercover: *Jun Takahaski, designer (spring/summer 2015)*. Coat Dress: *Alexander McQueen, designer (autumn/winter,1997-98)*.

Ensemble: *Jean Paul Gautier, designer (spring/summer 1994)*.

Dress: *Azzedine Alaia, designer (1992-95)*.

Ensemble: *Rick Owens, designer*
(autumn/winter 2015-16)

Evening Ensemble: *Pierpaolo Piccioli and Grazia Churri, designers*
(autumn/winter 2015-2016.)

Cocktail Dress: *Gabrielle "Coco" Chanel, designer*
(spring/summer 1960).

Ensemble: *A.F. Vandervorst and Filip Aricks, designers*
(autumn/winter 2001-2002).

Wedding Ensemble: *Cristobel Balenciaga, designer (1967).*

Wedding Ensemble: *Tom Browne, designer*
(2018).

Ensemble: *Tom Browne, designer*
(autumn/winter 2011-12).

Evening Ensemble: *Pierpaolo Picciola, designer*
(autumn/winter, 2017-18).

Evening Ensemble: *John Galliano, designer*
(autumn/winter 2000- 2001)

Evening Dress: *Alexander McQueen, designer*
(autumn/winter 2010-2011).

Evening Dress: *Dominico Dolce and Stephano Gabbana, designers*
(autumn/winter 2013-14).

Dress: *Alexander McQueen, designer*
(autumn /winter 2010-2011).

Evening Dress: *Oliver Theyskens, designer (spring/summer 1999).*

Breastplate: *Alexander Mc Queen and Shaun Leane, designers (spring/summer 2000).*

Evening Dress: *Grazia Churri and Pierpaola Picciolo, designers (spring/ summer, 2014).*

Evening Dress: *Pierpaolo Piccioli, designer (autumn /winter 2017-18.)*

Statuary Vestment for the Madonna Della Grazie: *Poor Benedictine Nuns of Lecce, designers (1950).*

Language in Evening Dress *Pierpaolo Piccioli, designer (autumn /winter 2017-18)* was borrowed from The Rite of Ordination of Catholic Bishops.

Photos of some of the couture can be found at:
https://www.metmuseum.org/exhibitions/listings/2018/heavenly-bodies

SOURCES

"1,659,647 Visitors to Costume Institute's *Heavenly Bodies* Show at Met Fifth Avenue and Met Cloisters Make It the Most Visited Exhibition in The Met's History." *The Metropolitan Museum of Art*, 2018, p.1. www.metmuseum.org/press/news/2018/heavenly-bodies-most-visited-exhibition

Bolton, Andrew. Katerina Jebb, illustrator. *Heavenly Bodies I: The Vatican Collection Fashion and the Catholic Imagination.* Yale University Press, 2018.

Bolton, Andrew. Katerina Jebb, illustrator. *Heavenly Bodies II Fashioning Worship III Fashioning Devotion. Fashion and the Catholic Imagination.* Yale University Press, 2018.

Joncas, Jan Michael. "Rite of Ordination of a Bishop (1968)." *Christian Worship Texts*, 1969, pp. 1-8. *courseweb.stthomas.edu/jmjoncas/.../Texts/.../Rite of Ordination of a Bishop.htm*

Nunez, Robert. "Reviving Catholic Manhood at Call to Chivalry Camp." *TFP Student Action*, 21 June 2018, www.tfpstudentaction.org/get-involved/call-to-chivalry-camps/catholic-manhood

Nussman, David. "Hundred Protest Blasphemous Met Exhibit." *Church Militant*, 12 June 2018, pp. 1-6. www.churchmilitant.com/news/article/faithful-catholics-protest-blasphemous-met-exhibit

"Lay Catholics Reject *Heavenly Bodies* Exhibit in NYC."
America Needs Fatima, 2018.
https://americaneedsfatima.org/Rally-News/realcatholics-reject-heavenly-bodies-exhibit-in-nyc.html

"Shaun Leane at Savage Beauty - Creating the 'Crown of Thorns' for Alexander McQueen."

YouTube, uploaded by Shaun Leane, 17 November 2017
https://www.youtube.com/watch?v=P1eXE8V-87o

ABOUT THE AUTHOR

Ellen Devlin is the author of two chapbooks, *Rita* (2019), and *Heavenly Bodies at the MET* (2023). Her poems can be found in *The Cortland Review, Ekphrasis, Lime Hawk Review, PANK, The New Ohio Review, The Sow's Ear* and *Women's Studies Quarterly Review.* and other journals, most recently *Beyond Words*, 2023, *Muleskinner* 2023, and *The Westchester Review*, 2023. She lives in Irvington, New York with her husband, Charles.

www.ingramcontent.com/pod-product-compliance
Lightning Source LLC
LaVergne TN
LVHW011414080426
835511LV00005B/540